"Until he extends the circle of his compassion to all living things, man will not himself find peace."

Albert Schweitzer

Dedicated to the loving spirit of my grandfather,
who inspired me to love nature and animals,
and shared the joy of raising a pet rabbit, Candy together.

Permission of Use Statement

The intent of this resource is for parents to use in their own private homes and/or teachers and child care professionals in their classrooms and professional settings.

Permission is granted to photocopy pages from this book only for those purposes.

The exercises in this book are gentle and safe provided the instructions are followed carefully. The authors disclaim all liability in connection with the use of the information in individual cases. If you have any doubts as to the suitability of the exercises, please consult a doctor. No part of this book should be construed as medical advice. Readers are expected to follow recommendations and make allowances for differences in children's abilities and physical conditions.

Calm Cottontails
Contents

Calm Cottontails
Introduction

Calm Cottontails is a program for parents, teachers, childcare professionals, yoga instructors, and anyone who loves children and wants to make a difference in their life. It's a program that focuses on a child's mind, body and spirit - bringing calmness and confidence at an early age. The program is geared for children ages 3-10.

Calm Cottontail lives in a peaceful garden and is a wonderful role model of calmness through the appreciation of nature. In 10 easy to follow lesson plans, many challenging behaviors can be addressed:

- Hyperactivity
- Sleep Problems
- Anger
- Anxiety
- Fears
- Loneliness
- Sadness
- Low Self-Esteem
- Lack of Focus
- Bad Days

Calm Cottontail will provide daily exercises that can be integrated into any daily routine. They provide innovative, creative and fun strategies that will help children find their calm place in any setting.

In a world of noise, stress, and pressure for young ones, it is our sincere desire, that Calm Cottontails will provide a positive, uplifting outlet for all children.

Calm Cottontails
Author's Message

I wanted to take this opportunity to share a personal message on how Calm Cottontails came into being…as a way to help parents and teachers understand what a strong impact they can have sharing these tools with their young children.

As a child, I struggled with severe anxiety and difficulty sleeping and calming myself. I had a favorite book that I would look at each evening – it had a picture of a little girl sleeping so contently in a bed. I remember thinking, she looked so peaceful and calm – and my sincerest desire was to be like her. Every night at bedtime, I would look at that picture for a very long time, thinking of it as I tried to go to sleep. That vision is still so strong in my mind today – and reminds me of the huge importance visual images can have in our lives.

As I developed into an adult and continued to struggle with anxiety, calming benefits of yoga, breathing, visualization, and nature all played a huge effect on ultimately diminishing these challenges within myself.

As I become a mother and had a daughter, who was extremely active, I wanted to learn all the tools that could help encourage calming and confidence. As I watched her grow and have challenges in school and settings that required quiet, calm behavior, I realized how many children around the world are dealing with the same issues – with frustrated parents and teachers.

While I believe Calm Cottontails can help all children – I have a special place in my heart for children who are extremely active and dealing with special challenges.

I believe this program can give them the tools they need to find calmness and confidence. It is my sincere desire that spending time in their peaceful garden each day with Calm Cottontail will make a positive change in their lives.

I wish you all the best in your endeavors helping the children in your life.

Many blessings,

Christi
Christi Eley, Author Calm Cottontails
Founder, Angel Bear Yoga®

<u>Calm Cottontails</u>
Mission Statement

We sit and walk in calmness in our garden…

Our garden is a safe place…it's also enchanted, which means wonderful things can happen here…

We do no harm in our garden – to ourselves or others…

We always come from a place of calm love and compassion – for ourselves and others…

We know that we can find calmness and peace at anytime when we come to our garden…

We will take this calmness & peace out into the world and spread it for all to see…

Calm Cottontails
Moonlit Garden Space

Set aside one area in your home or classroom that will be a peaceful, safe place –
that can be the child's very own Moonlit Garden Space. They can go to this special
place anytime they are showing signs of needing to find calmness and peace.

You will want to place items that appeal to a child's visual, auditory and
kinesthetic senses. Here are some ideas:

Visual:
- Bunny Photos/Decorations
- Moon/Celestial Photos/Decorations
- Flow Photos/Decorations
- Soft Lighting

Auditory:
- CD Player
    o Nature CD's, Soothing Music CD's
    o We recommend the following CD's:
        ▪ "Sounds of the Night" & "The Garden" (www.oreade.com)

Kinesthetic:
- Soft Rug
- Comfy Pillow
- Stuffed Animals

Another wonderful idea is to take the child on a nature walk. Have them gather
"treasures" that they can put in their special spot to remind them of their
peaceful garden.

Here are products that would be wonderful in your space:

1. Constellation Ladybug Light
   www.chinaberry.com

2. Lavender Wands
   www.caroleesherfarm.com

<u>Calm Cottontails</u>
Be Creative – Have Fun!

There are many ways to add creativity to the lesson plans. We want you and your child to have fun and let your minds be free!

Animals:
- Find real photos of all the animals in the program to share with the children. They love seeing these photos and you can post them in your special Moonlit Garden Space.
- Expand the lessons by finding out more information on the new animal friend – read books, draw pictures, play games all related to this animal.

Flowers:
- Find real photos of all the flowers in the program to share with the children. This will be a wonderful visual cue as you're doing your breathing exercises.
- Planting some real flowers inside or outside will bring beauty and a calming atmosphere to your child.

Coloring:
- After each session, have the child color their flower photo and their cottontail stretch photo.
- They can create their own special book with these drawings – color the front page as their cover.

Share:
- Parents and teachers can share their own personal stories on how they bring calmness and confidence into their lives.
- For example, share with your child – what you find beautiful in the world, your comfy place, your favorite thing to listen to. This will help them by giving them ideas and making them more comfortable in the process.

Calm Cottontails
Animal & Flower Photos

We recommend printing out real photos of the animals and flowers for the lesson plans. The children love seeing the real photos and they are wonderful visual cues. For the flowers, you can just google search their name and many photos will come up.

For the animals, we are listing very good website for photos.

1. Hedgehog
   http://curiousanimals.net/funnies-bunnies/creature-feature-hedgehogs-funny-facts/

2. Fireflies
   http://mycrossstitchpatterns.com/images/Beautiful%20Purple%20Dragonfly.jpg
   http://pkukmweb.ukm.my/~hutan/photos/dragonfly02.jpg

3. Meadow Vole
   http://www.nenature.com/Images/MeadowVoleLAT.jpg

4. Lightning Bug
   http://chessaleeinlondon.files.wordpress.com/2008/04/firefly.jpg

5. Ladybug
   http://farm1.static.flickr.com/32/50833605_5013d78751.jpg
   http://farm4.static.flickr.com/3170/2505261503_08f4bee022.jpg

6. Nightingale Bird
   http://a-z-animals.com/images/animals/nightingale1_large.jpg

7. Barn Owl
   http://www.nhptv.org/natureworks/barnowl.htm

8. Hummingbird Moth
   http://karennovak.files.wordpress.com/2007/06/hummingbird-hawk-moth.jpg

9. Luna Moth
   http://farm1.static.flickr.com/95/247991589_b8777004dc.jpg

10. Mockingbird
    http://seabournrocks.pbworks.com/f/1220922232/mockingbird.jpg

Calm Cottontails
When To Use

It is recommended to be consistent and set-up a regular time of day where you go to your peaceful garden to see Calm Cottontail. Children will find great comfort in knowing that they have a specific time each day where they can do this. For example, parents may choose evening an ideal time – right before bedtime for calming benefits. Teachers, on the other hand, may choose first thing in the morning to set the tone for the day. Of course, you can add in other times during the day as needed for calming benefits.

There are 10 lesson plans in this program. Depending on what challenges the child may be having, you can choose which lesson plan would be most beneficial.

1. Hyperactivity   Patience Lesson Plan
                                     Peace Lesson Plan

2. Lack of Focus   Listening Lesson Plan

3. Sad, Worried   Comfort Lesson Plan
                                     Beauty Lesson Plan

4. Bad Day, Things Didn't Go Well   Acceptance Lesson Plan

5. Anger   Love Lesson Plan

6. Low Self-Esteem, Negativity   Thoughts Lesson Plan
                                     Gratitude Lesson Plan
                                     Beauty Lesson Plan

7. Forgiveness, Loneliness,
   Getting Along with Other   Courtesy Lesson Plan

8. Anxiety/Stress   Peace Lesson Plan
                                     Comfort Lesson Plan

Calm Cottontails
How To Use

Calm Cottontails was designed to be easy to use, adaptable to any environment, and a program that anyone could follow along with. There are 10 simple lesson plans that are broken down into 10 exercises. It is recommended to do the exercises throughout the day in small amounts, so that the child has repeated reminders throughout the day for ways to relax and calm.

Exercise #1 – Entering the Peaceful Garden
The first exercise in each lesson plan is a way to initially have the child sit, close their eyes and find their peaceful place. If you have a lavender wand, this can be a wonderful tool to initiate the wonder of going to this imaginary place. Just wave the lavender wand around each time you want to instill calm – you can also have the children do their breathing exercises by breathing in the beautiful fragrance of the wand.
When To Use:
This should be done when you're ready to start a lesson.

Exercise #2 – Bunny Breath Breaths
The second exercise is breathing. This may be the single most important tool in helping children find inner calmness. Encourage the children to take a big breath from down deep in their bellies. Then exhale fully through their mouth. They can stay seating with their legs crossed or get up on their knees and flow up and down while inhaling and exhaling.
When To Use:
This can be done any time of day and should be encouraged multiple times throughout the day. Obtain photos of the flower from the Internet or a book.

Exercise #3 – Calm Cottontail Stretch
The third exercise is stretching time. This is a wonderful way for children to get their energy/activity out in a healthy, positive way. Children also learn best by movement, so by encouraging these stretches and talking about their meaning, children have a better idea of the concepts you are introducing. Remember you can do more then one stretch at a time if the child is very active and you want some good exercise time.
When To Use:
Any time during the day when the child is very active.

Exercise #4 – Bunny Whisperer

The fourth exercise introduces a new animal friend each time. This is to foster an interest in nature and animals, which is very calming and also to foster an attitude of compassion for all living creatures. Being a Bunny Whisperer and encouraging very quiet, soothing voices is a very positive step in teaching children that they can calm themselves.

When To Use:

When you want to encourage the child to speak softly, and in a kind voice. Obtain photos of animal friend from the Internet or a book to share with child.

Exercise #5 – Bridge of Dreams

The fifth exercise is teaching children to make an active decision – to leave their problems behind, and take the step (across the bridge) to new calming, positive thoughts and behaviors. The children can use their imagination by creating a Midnight Tea Party – with real friends or imaginary friends.

When To Use:

When the child is having a challenging time dealing with an issue. Just let them know that they can leave their challenges behind at the bridge...and don't move on to the next activity until they do so.

Exercise #6 – Moonbeam Rides

The sixth exercise is an extremely important message – teaching the child that they do have control over their emotions – the can choose to change the way they are feeling at any moment. By watching Calm Cottontail change his tail color and the moonbeam changing color, it proves to be wonderful visualization to this concept. This is especially helpful if your child is a visual learner.

When To Use:

You can encourage this by providing pompoms or something of the same color as a visual reminder throughout the day. This encourages the child that they are capable of changing their emotions.

Exercise #7 – Moonlight Serenade

The seventh exercise encourages positive affirmations in the way of a song (so that you are being like the birds in the garden). Saying these positive affirmations over and over again, help the child to understand the concept even more – especially if they are an auditory learner. Using the visual cue of looking for the Bunny Blossoms during the day will encourage the child to see the positives.

When To Use:

You can say these at any time during the day.

Calm Cottontails
How To Use

Exercise #8 – Landing Back in the Peaceful Garden
The eighth exercise is a final relaxation time with a beautiful guided imagery. It is recommended to use an eye pillow, which will help the child to fully relax and not be distracted.
When To Use:
When you want the child to sit or lay down for a few moments.

Exercise #9 – Bunny Hugs
The ninth exercise is promoting love and compassion. Having the child hug a stuffed animal that can represent Calm Cottontail, or a real pet animal can be extremely comforting and therapeutic. Giving other people hugs is also awesome!
When To Use:
Anytime during the day!

Exercise #10 – Courage
The tenth exercise is showing the child that they can do anything! It takes great courage to learn these lessons and follow through with them – to work through your fears and challenges. By affirming this and doing the Courage Stretch, the child will gain confidence.
When To Use:
When the child is showing fear or lack of confidence.

Quick Calming Tips
The quick calming tips are very easy, fast ways that you can use these lesson plans in small amounts during the day. It is not necessary to read through the entire lesson plan or exercise – just by doing these quick calming tips, you can help your child throughout the day in any setting.

Calm Cottontails
Recommended Bunny Books

We have a collection of bunny books that I would recommend integrating into this program. Taking time to read greatly calms children down before facilitating a lesson plan exercise.

1. Rabbits & Raindrops
    By: Jim Arnosky
    ISBN# 0-698-11815-4
    Message - the beauty of nature and taking time to experience it.
    Lesson Plan – Acceptance

2. Hugs on the Wind
    By: Marsha Diane Arnold & Vernise Elaine Pelzel
    ISBN# 0-8109-5968-2
    Message – Missing someone and how nature can help
    Lesson Plan - Comfort

3. Little Bunny's Sleepless Night
    By: Carol Roth
    ISBN# 0-7358-1069-9
    Message – Finding comfort & ways to fall asleep
    Lesson Plan - Comfort

4. Tell Me Something Happy Before I Go To Sleep
    By: Joyce Dunbar
    ISBN# 0-15-201795-X
    Message – Thinking happy thoughts before bedtime
    Lesson Plan – Thoughts

5. Quiet Bunny
    By: Lisa McCue
    ISBN# 978-1-4027-5719-8
    Message – Self-esteem – being happy with who we are
    Lesson Plan - Gratitude

6. While We Were Out
    By: Ho Baek Lee
    ISBN# 1-929132-44-1
    Message - Imagination and humor.
    Lesson Plan – Beauty

7. The Country Bunny and the Little Gold Shoes
   By: Du Bose Heyward
   ISBN# 978-0395185575
   Message – Self-esteem - having dreams and believing in yourself
   Lesson Plan - Patience

8. I Will Kiss You
   By: Stoo Hample
   ISBN# 076362787-9
   Message – Love
   Lesson Plan - Love

9. It's Not Easy Being A Bunny
   By: Marilyn Sadler
   ISBN# 0-394-86102-7
   Message – Self-esteem – being happy with yourself
   Lesson Plan – Acceptance

10. Little Bunny Kung Fu
    By: Regan Johnson
    ISBN# 0-9769417-8-3
    Message – Respect for nature
    Lesson Plan – Peace

11. Mr. Rabbit and the Lovely Present
    By: Charlotte Zolotow
    ISBN# 0-06-026945-6
    Message – The joy of giving
    Lesson Plan – Courtesy

12. Doctor Rabbit's Foundling
    By: Ian Wahl
    ISBN# 0-671-69008-6
    Message – Compassion for living creatures
    Lesson Plan - Love

Calm Cottontail
Acceptance Lesson Plan

Exercise #1
Entering the Peaceful Garden

- Sit with legs crossed and eyes closed.
- Use Lavender Wand

We're getting ready to enter our peaceful garden….close your eyes, relax and just sit back…we don't know what's going to happen in our garden today, but we must accept anything that comes our way.

Calm Cottontail is going to meet us in the garden. Rabbits must accept the fact that they are very small and are sometimes chased by other animals. They accept this and are still happy and calm in their garden…they find safe places to hide and enjoy being small and getting to see small areas of the garden.

Say together:
"I am going to my peaceful garden where I will accept anything that comes my way."

Calm Cottontail
Acceptance Lesson Plan

Exercise #2
Bunny Breath Breaths

• **Sit with their legs crossed or on knees.**

Calm Cottontail is sitting under the Peacock Orchid flower. This is a very tall blooming flower – it can reach 40 inches tall! It's a beautiful white flower with a purple center.

Calm Cottontail loves looking up at this amazing flower – sometimes it gives him shade when he sits under it since he's so small. By doing your breathing under this flower, you can accept anything that comes your way.

Breath in – I accept all things that come to me.
Breath out – I know that I have everything I need at this moment.

• Repeat breathing 5-10 times…slow & deep

Other Breathing Suggestions:
• Have children just think happy thoughts as they do their breathing – don't accept any unhappy thoughts today!
• Each time they breathe in, have them think a happy thought, and as they breathe out, have them send this happy thought out to the world.

Calm Cottontail
Acceptance Lesson Plan

Exercise #3
Calm Cottontail Stretch

• Get comfortable – remove shoes and be on a nonslid surface.

Calm Cottontail is going to show you how to take time to accept all things in your life.

Instructions for the stretch:
Sit on the floor with legs crossed. Place hands on the ground behind you. Look up slowly and stretch back – chest rising upward. Then slowly bring arms in front of you, folding them on the ground and resting your head down.

• Rest in this pose for 10 seconds to start…then longer.

As you do this stretch, imagine sitting with Calm Cottontail in the middle of your garden. As you look up, you see clouds and feel some raindrops. At first, you are upset, but Calm Cottontail says the rain can be beautiful. You both find a soft spot under the Peacock Orchid flower – it's like an umbrella to you! You both sit and watch the rain come down. As you do, you are enjoying the quiet time – and you feel so peaceful and calm.

Calm Cottontails
Acceptance Lesson Plan

Exercise #4
Bunny Whisperer

- Sit in a comfortable position.

Calm Cottontail wants to introduce you to his friend, the Hedgehog. This is an amazing creature...so very small, but it has very sharp spines to protect them. Even though they are small, they accept this and learn to do amazing things – they can climb trees and swim! They also make interesting sounds and have an amazing sense of smell!

- Show the child a photo of a real hedgehog.

- Have children close their eyes.

Calm Cottontail says that you can learn to talk to all of his friends in the Peaceful Garden...that you can become the Bunny Whisperer. All you have to do is keep your eyes closed, imagine walking up to the Hedgehog. What would you like to ask him? Take a long look at him – what would you like to name him?

- Practice talking like the Bunny Whisperer... What would you like to talk about today?

Calm Cottontails
Acceptance Lesson Plan

Exercise #5
Bridge of Dreams

- Sit with legs crossed and eyes closed.

Calm Cottontail shows you the bridge of dreams…it is here that you can ask for anything. Keep your eyes closed and think about what you want to wish for today….

Before you can walk across the bridge, you must promise to accept anything that comes you way – you don't know what will happen today, but you agree to make the best of anything that happens. You can always make it a great day! You new friend, Hedgehog is walking next to you.

When you get to the other side of the bridge, you all celebrate by dancing in the moonlight – Calm Cottontail loves to dance when he's happy! Kick up those big feet and jump all around!

- To have some fun, you can dance around the room – it will feel good!

- You can also have a Midnight Tea Party – who would you invite?

Calm Cottontails
Acceptance Lesson Plan

Exercise #6
Moonbeam Rides

- **Sit with legs crossed and eyes closed.**

The peaceful garden is turning purple...keep your eyes closed and imagine seeing this color all around you. As you look at Calm Cottontail, he is also changing – his cottontail is turning purple – can you see it? This reminds us, that we can also change – we can change how we feel at any moment. Right now, let's open our mind to acceptance...knowing we have everything we need at this moment.

You see a purple moonbeam coming your way – you, Calm Cottontail and Hedgehog all jump on. The next time things don't go your way, you don't get what you want, just remember that you can change your feelings...and you can accept anything that comes your way. You watch your problems disappear into the night sky...one by one. Close your eyes and watch this...

On the moonbeam is the softest bed of forest moss and beautiful ferns acting as a blanket. You lay your head down and Hedgehog is next to you. He is taking a rest on the Peacock Orchid flower and just resting next to you...you both feel very peaceful at this moment.

- **You can give the children a purple pompom, so they will remember to accept whatever comes.**

Calm Cottontail
Acceptance Lesson Plan

Exercise #7
Moonlight Serenade

- Sit in a comfortable position.

As the moonbeam goes over the trees, you hear the music of the night – birds singing, crickets chirping – take time to listen. It's like a beautiful Moonlight Serenade.

- It's your turn to sing now:

    "I accept all that comes to me." "I accept all that comes to me."
  Can you hear the birds singing it with you?

You can sing this serenade anytime you are lonely or don't know what to say to someone. By singing this song, you are sending peace out to the whole world.

Bunny Blossoms
Every time you sing this song, it wakes up all of the flowers in the garden. And if you look very closely, you can see them all turning into Bunny Blossoms – they are all taking the shape of little bunnies...and showing you that anything is possible!

- Play a nature CD for relaxation at this time.

Calm Cottontail
Acceptance Lesson Plan

Exercise #8
Landing back in the Enchanted Garden

• Lay down with eye pillow.

You smell the Peacock Orchid flower again – breathe in the beautiful fragrance, breathe out into the night sky.

Sometimes we are disappointed when things don't go our way, but we can always turn things around.

Let's take a walk in our peaceful garden. As you walk further into the garden on this lovely evening, you find yourself in a magnificent field of flowers. As you look around, you see every color and type of flower ever created. They are all so beautiful and filling the air with a beautiful smell. You want to pick one for yourself, so you look around to find just the perfect one. You take a long time to decide – and finally you see the one just for you. You reach down to grab it, and instead grab the flower next to it. At first, you are disappointed, as it's not the one you originally wanted. As you hold it in your hands, it begins to light up, and before you know it, it's amazing light is shining all over the entire garden. You realize that it's the most perfect flower for you. You place it in a safe place to keep forever. You realize that you must accept all gifts that are given to you – as they all serve a purpose and are the perfect gifts for you.

Calm Cottontail
Acceptance Lesson Plan

Exercise #9
Bunny Hugs

- Have a Calm Cottontail Bunny with you now.

Everything around you is just perfect – you have accepted everything that came your way. Calm Cottontail helped you and you're going to give him a big Bunny Hug now.

You might want to give someone else a big Bunny Hug…can you think of anyone?

Exercise #10
Courage

It takes great courage to learn something new…and do something that is very difficult. By doing this lesson, you had great courage and Calm Cottontail and your new friend, Hedgehog are very proud of you!

Do the Courage Stretch – be proud!!!!

Calm Cottontail
Acceptance Lesson Plan

Quick Calming Tips

Lavender Wand
When you wave the lavender wand, children will know it's time to have acceptance.

Bunny Breath Breaths
These can be done anytime, anywhere. Have children close their eyes and imagine that they are breathing in the Peacock Orchid flower.

Calm Cottontail Stretch
Take time to do the Calm Cottontail Acceptance Stretch during the day.

Bunny Whisperer
Remember to accept everything today. Think of your friend, the Hedgehog.

Bridge of Dreams
Remember to leave your problems behind before you move on.

Moonbeam Rides
Give children a purple pompom to remind them of them acceptance today.

Moonlight Serenades
Take time to listen to Nature CD and say your affirmation throughout the day. "I accept all that comes to me." Look for the Bunny Blossoms.

Calm Cottontail Bunny
Let's sit with Calm Cottontail – we both will be accepting.
Hold Calm Cottontail and give him a Bunny Hug.

Courage
Take time to do the courage stretch whenever you are feeling worried or scared. Remember you can do anything!

Acceptance (A)

Acceptance (B)

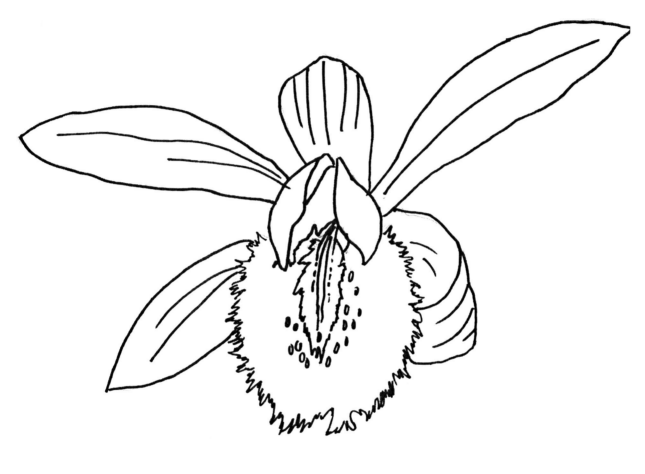

PEACOCK ORCHID

Calm Cottontail
Beauty Lesson Plan

Exercise #1
Entering the Peaceful Garden

- Sit with legs crossed and eyes closed.
- Use Lavender Wand

We're getting ready to enter our peaceful garden....close your eyes, relax and just sit back. There is so much beauty around us in the garden – just looking at it makes us feel better.

Calm Cottontail is going to meet us in the garden. Rabbits are such beautiful creatures – they make people smile and feel good because they are so adorable and interesting. When we look at them, we are reminded that all creatures are beautiful and bring so much happiness to the world.

Say together:
"I am going to my peaceful garden where I will take time to see the beauty around me and inside me."

Calm Cottontail
Beauty Lesson Plan

Exercise #2
Bunny Breath Breaths

- Sit with their legs crossed or on knees.

Calm Cottontail is sitting under the Ludwigia Peruviana flower. It's also called the "Primrose Willow" flower. It's a beautiful bright yellow flower that lights up the whole garden.

Calm Cottontail says that when we notice these bright beautiful things – it lights up our whole life.

Breath in – I am opening my eyes to see.
Breath out – I see all the beauty around me – filling my life with wonder.

- Repeat breathing 5-10 times...slow & deep

Other Breathing Suggestions:
- Each time, you take a breath – think of something you find beautiful.
- There are so many things – make a list!

Calm Cottontail
Beauty Lesson Plan

Exercise #3
Calm Cottontail Stretch

- Get comfortable – remove shoes and be on a nonslid surface.

Calm Cottontail is going to show you how you can take time to see all the beauty around you.

Instructions for the stretch:
Lay on stomach. Place hands next to you by shoulders. Use back muscles to help raise your head and upper back off the floor slowly while looking upward. Flow up and down several times. You can also turn to each side and look around while doing this stretch.

- Rest in this pose for 10 seconds to start…then longer.

As you do this stretch, imagine sitting with Calm Cottontail in the middle of your garden. Imagine you are both laying in the grass – looking up to see all the beautiful things around you. What do you see? Anytime you are feeling sad or upset, just look around and let the beauty shine on you.

Calm Cottontails
Beauty Lesson Plan

Exercise #4
Bunny Whisperer

- Sit in a comfortable position.

Calm Cottontail wants to introduce you to his friend, Dragonfly. Dragonflies are definitely one of the most beautiful creatures! They come in so many different colors – blue, green, red…and their wings seem to shimmer silver under the moonlight. They also help us by eating pesky mosquitoes when evening comes.

- Show the child a photo of a real Dragonfly.

- Have children close their eyes.

Calm Cottontail says that you can learn to talk to all of his friends in the Peaceful Garden…that you can become the Bunny Whisperer. All you have to do is keep your eyes closed, imagine walking up to the Dragonfly. What would you like to ask him? Take a long look at him – what would you like to name him? What color is your Dragonfly?

- Practice talking like the Bunny Whisperer… What would you like to talk about today?

Calm Cottontails
Beauty Lesson Plan

Exercise #5
Bridge of Dreams

- **Sit with legs crossed and eyes closed.**

Calm Cottontail shows you the bridge of dreams...it is here that you can ask for anything. Keep your eyes closed and think about what you want to wish for today....

Before you can walk across the bridge, you must promise to keep your eyes open and look for the beauty around you. You have to let go of any feelings of not liking yourself – you are beautiful inside and out. You new friend, Dragonfly is flying next to you.

When you get to the other side of the bridge, you all celebrate by dancing in the moonlight – Calm Cottontail loves to dance when he's happy! Kick up those big feet and jump all around!

- To have some fun, you can dance around the room – it will feel good!

- You can also have a <u>Midnight Tea Party</u> – who would you invite?

Calm Cottontails
Beauty Lesson Plan

Exercise #6
Moonbeam Rides

- Sit with legs crossed and eyes closed.

The peaceful garden is turning a beautiful color of fuchsia...keep your eyes closed and imagine seeing this color all around you. As you look at Calm Cottontail, he is also changing – his cottontail is turning fuchsia – can you see it? This reminds us, that we can also change – we can change how we feel at any moment. Right now, no matter what is going on in our lives, we can look inside and find so much beauty.

You see a fuchsia moonbeam coming your way – you, Calm Cottontail and Dragonfly all jump on. The next time you are feeling sad or upset, just find the beauty and you can watch your problems disappear into the night sky...one by one. Close your eyes and watch this...

On the moonbeam is the softest bed of forest moss and beautiful ferns acting as a blanket. You lay your head down and Dragonfly lands on the Primrose Willow Flower next to...you both feel very peaceful at this moment.

- You can give the children an fuchsia pompom, so they will remember to accept whatever comes.

Calm Cottontail
Beauty Lesson Plan

Exercise #7
Moonlight Serenade

- Sit in a comfortable position.

As the moonbeam goes over the trees, you hear the music of the night – birds singing, crickets chirping – take time to listen. It's like a beautiful Moonlight Serenade.

- It's your turn to sing now:

    "I see beauty." "I see beauty."
    "I am beautiful." "I am beautiful."
    Can you hear the birds singing it with you?

By singing this song, you are sending beauty out to the world.

Bunny Blossoms
Every time you sing this song, it wakes up all the flowers in the garden. And if you look very closely, you can see them all turning into Bunny Blossoms – they are all taking the shape of little bunnies...and showing you that anything is possible!

- Play a nature CD for relaxation at this time.

Calm Cottontail
Beauty Lesson Plan

Exercise #8
Landing back in the Enchanted Garden

- Lay down with eye pillow.

You smell the Primrose Willow flower again – breathe in the beautiful fragrance, breathe out into the night sky.

We must remember to take time very day to see the beauty around us...this will help us to see the beauty inside us as well. You are so beautiful and amazing!

As you walk around the garden tonight, the moon is shining so bright. It's lighting up so many beautiful things in the garden – everything looks so very special tonight. You look down and find a knapsack...it's also shining very brightly in the moonlight. As you pick it up and look inside, you see that's it's filled with many things. As you begin to pull things out, you realize that it's filled with everything that makes you beautiful and special. You realize that you carry around these things every day – and you can reach inside and see your beauty anytime you want. You are feeling so happy and peaceful, that you lay your head down under the Primrose Willow Flower and drift off to sleep with the beautiful dragonfly beside you.

Calm Cottontail
Beauty Lesson Plan

Exercise #9
Bunny Hugs

- Have a Calm Cottontail Bunny with you now.

There is so much beauty all around you...and you feel beautiful inside.
Calm Cottontail helped you and you're going to give him a big Bunny Hug now.

You might want to give someone else a big Bunny Hug...can you think of anyone?

Exercise #10
Courage

It takes great courage to learn something new...and do something that is very difficult. By doing this lesson, you had great courage and Calm Cottontail and your new friend, Dragonfly is very proud of you!

Do the Courage Stretch - be proud!!!!

Calm Cottontail
Beauty Lesson Plan

Quick Calming Tips

Lavender Wand
When you wave the lavender wand, children will know it's time to look for beauty around you and inside you.

Bunny Breath Breaths
These can be done anytime, anywhere. Have children close their eyes and imagine that they are breathing in the Primrose Willow Flower.

Calm Cottontail Stretch
Take time to do the Calm Cottontail Beauty Stretch during the day.

Bunny Whisperer
Remember to take time to look for beauty today. Think of your friend, the Dragonfly.

Bridge of Dreams
Remember to leave your problems behind before you move on.

Moonbeam Rides
Give children a fuchsia pompom to remind them to find beauty today.

Moonlight Serenades
Take time to listen to Nature CD and say your affirmation throughout the day. "I am beautiful." Remember to always look for the Bunny Blossoms.

Calm Cottontail Bunny
Let's sit with Calm Cottontail – we both will look for the beauty.
Hold Calm Cottontail and give him a Bunny Hug.

Courage
Take time to do the courage stretch when you are feeling worried or scared. Remember you can do anything!

Beauty

LUDWIGIA PERUVIANA

<u>Calm Cottontail</u>
Comfort Lesson Plan

<u>Exercise #1</u>
Entering the Peaceful Garden

- **Sit with legs crossed and eyes closed.**
- **Use Lavender Wand**

We're getting ready to enter our peaceful garden….close your eyes, relax and let your thoughts be peaceful. We are choosing to find comfort in this special place…to a place where we can feel happy and peaceful.

Calm Cottontail is going to meet us in the garden. Do you know how he feels comfort…he digs burrows deep in the ground and makes a safe, happy place to sleep. He wants to show you his special place. As soon as you are quite, peaceful and comforted, he will appear to you.

- Say together:
  "I am going to my peaceful garden where I will find comfort."

Calm Cottontail
Comfort Lesson Plan

Exercise #2
Bunny Breath Breaths

- **Sit with their legs crossed or on knees.**

Calm Cottontail is sitting under the Tuberose Flower waiting for you.
This flower is found in Mexico. It has very unique white petals. Its fragrance is so spectacular, they use it in many perfumes.

Calm Cottontail teaches us how to breathe...rabbits are constantly moving their noses, this is one way they are able to take in more air – and be happy!

Breath in – smell this lovely flower and feel happiness...
Breath out – sending away all sad or worried feelings...blowing them into the night air...

- Repeat breathing 5-10 times...slow & deep

Other Breathing Suggestions:
- Breathe in while counting to 5 and exhale while counting to 5.

Calm Cottontail
Comfort Lesson Plan

Exercise #3
Calm Cottontail Stretch

- Get comfortable – remove shoes and be on a nonslid surface.

Calm Cottontail is going to show you how he touches the ground and finds comfort.

Instructions for the stretch:
Sit on knees. Fold body over knees, gently bending down to the ground. See how far you can go…can you place your forehead down on the floor. Extend arms straight out overhead touching the ground.

- Rest in this pose for 10 seconds to start…then longer.

As you do this stretch, imagine Calm Cottontail taking you to see his burrow – he's showing you all around…imagine what would be underground…down the rabbit hole.

- Ask the children questions: What does his Calm Cottontail's home look like? How does it feel down there? Do you want to stay?

Calm Cottontails
Comfort Lesson Plan

Exercise #4
Bunny Whisperer

- Sit in a comfortable position.

Calm Cottontail wants to introduce us to his friend, the Meadow Vole.
The meadow vole is another amazing animal that loves to dig burrows in the ground. He feels comfort under the ground and wants to show you his home.

- Show the child a photo of a real Meadow Vole.

- Have children close their eyes.

Calm Cottontail says that you can learn to talk to all of his friends in the Peaceful Garden...that you can become the Bunny Whisperer. All you have to do is keep your eyes closed, imagine walking up to the Meadow Vole, and in a very soft, calm voice talk to him...what would you like to say, do you have any questions for him? You can give him a name...what would you like to call him?

- Practice talking like the Bunny Whisperer... What would you like to talk about today?

Calm Cottontails
Comfort Lesson Plan

Exercise #5
Bridge of Dreams

- Sit with legs crossed and eyes closed.

Calm Cottontail shows you the bridge of dreams…it is here that you can ask for anything. Keep your eyes closed and think about what you want to wish for today….

Before you can walk across the bridge, you must leave all your problems behind…if you are feeling sad or unhappy, leave these feelings behind. Think of a place where you feel comfort - a special place that makes you feel warm and safe and happy. As you begin to walk across the bridge, all of your problems are floating down the river under you…can you see them floating by? On the other side of the bride, your new, special friend is waiting for you - the Meadow Vole.

When you get to the other side of the bridge, you all celebrate by dancing in the moonlight - Calm Cottontail loves to dance when he's happy!

- To have some fun, you can dance around the room - it will feel good!

- You can have a <u>Midnight Tea Party</u> - who would you like to invite?

Calm Cottontails
Comfort Lesson Plan

Exercise #6
Moonbeam Rides

- **Sit with legs crossed and eyes closed.**

The peaceful garden is turning Dark Blue…keep your eyes closed and imagine seeing this color all around you. As you look at Calm Cottontail, he is also changing – his cottontail is turning dark blue – can you see it? This reminds us, that we can also change – we can change how we feel at any moment. Right now, let's not feel sad, let's feel comfort and happiness.

You see a dark blue moonbeam coming your way – you, Calm Cottontail and Meadow Vole all jump on. All your sadness and unhappiness goes away and you are left with feeling comfort and happiness. You watch your problems disappear into the night sky…one by one. Close your eyes and watch this…

On the moonbeam is the softest bed of forest moss and beautiful ferns acting as a blanket. You lay your head down and feel such comfort…you feel so safe and so loved. You could stay here for a long time.

- **You can give the children a blue pom pom, so they will remember that comfort is all around them today…**

Calm Cottontail
Comfort Lesson Plan

Exercise #7
Moonlight Serenade

- Sit in a comfortable position.

As the moonbeam goes over the trees, you hear the music of the night – birds singing, crickets chirping – take time to listen. It's like a beautiful Moonlight Serenade.

- It's your turn to sing now:

    "I feel comfort, I feel comfort."
    Can you hear the birds singing it with you?

You can sing this serenade anytime you are feeling sad, worried or upset.
By being calm, you are sending peace out to the whole world.

Bunny Blossoms
Every time you sing this song, it wakes up all of the flowers in the garden. And if you look very closely, you can see them all turning into Bunny Blossoms – they are all taking the shape of little bunnies...and showing you that anything is possible!

- Play a nature CD for relaxation at this time.

48

Calm Cottontail
Comfort Lesson Plan

Exercise #8
Landing back in the Enchanted Garden

• Lay down with eye pillow.

You smell the Tuberose flower again – breathe in the beautiful fragrance, breathe out into the night sky. You are tired and want to lie down after your moonbeam ride. You lay your head down and find yourself laying on a beautiful cloud that's landed in the garden. It feels so soft and comfortable. You hear a waterfall behind you, and the trickling sound of water makes you very sleepy. You feel the soft touch of Calm Cottontail as he lays down next to you. He loves to be close to you. You keep your eyes close and know that you are well taken care of, you have much love around you, and feel very comforted. This place feels like home.

Calm Cottontail
Comfort Lesson Plan

Exercise #9
Bunny Hugs

- Have a Calm Cottontail Bunny with you now.

You are filled with comfort and love now...Calm Cottontail helped you and you're going to give him a big Bunny Hug now.

You might want to give someone else a big Bunny Hug...can you think of anyone?

Exercise #10
Courage

It takes great courage to learn something new...and do something that is very difficult. By doing this lesson, you had great courage and Calm Cottontail and your new friend, Meadow Vole are very proud of you!

Do the Courage Stretch - be proud!!!!

Calm Cottontail
Comfort Lesson Plan

Quick Calming Tips

Lavender Wand
When you wave the lavender wand, children will know it's time to go their peaceful garden and think about their favorite comfy place.

Bunny Breaths
These can be done anytime, anywhere. Have children close their eyes and imagine that they are breathing in the Tuberose flower.

Calm Cottontail Stretch
Take time to do the Calm Cottontail Comfort Stretch during the day.

Bunny Whisperer
Remember to talk quietly and calmly at all times…this will spread comfort to all those around you. Think of your friend, the Meadow Vole.

Bridge of Dreams
Remember to leave your problems behind before you move on.

Moonbeam Rides
Give children a blue pompom to remind them of comfort during the day.

Moonlight Serenades
Take time to listen to Nature CD and say affirmation throughout the day.
"I feel comfort. I feel comfort." Look for the Bunny Blossoms.

Calm Cottontail Bunny
It's time to send Calm Cottontail comfort…send him comforting thoughts.
Hold Calm Cottontail and give him a Bunny Hug.

Courage
Take time to do the courage stretch whenever you are feeling worried or scared. Remember you can do anything!

Comfort

TUBEROSE

Calm Cottontail
Courtesy Lesson Plan

Exercise #1
Entering the Peaceful Garden

- Sit with legs crossed and eyes closed.
- Use Lavender Wand

We're getting ready to enter our peaceful garden....close your eyes, relax and bring loving thoughts into your heart. There are so many people who care about you...we're going to send them loving thoughts right now.

Calm Cottontail is going to meet us in the garden. Did you know that rabbits have personality! That means every rabbit acts their own way...some are quiet, some are fast, some like to play games. The one thing they all have in common is that they all like being treated nice...they love when people are gentle and kind to them. This is called showing courtesy – using manners and treating everyone with respect. We should show courtesy to all living creatures and all people.

- Say together:
  "I am going to my peaceful garden where I will be nice to everyone around me."

Calm Cottontail
Courtesy Lesson Plan

Exercise #2
Bunny Breath Breaths

- Sit with their legs crossed or on knees.

Calm Cottontail is sitting under the Night Scented Stock flower. This is a delicate, small flower that only grows six inches tall. It can be white, pink or lavender in color and it has the sweetest fragrance.

Calm Cottontail is moving his nose very fast. That happens when he gets nervous. He said someone wasn't very nice to him and his nose is twitching fast. Let's calm it down by doing our breathing.

Breath in – smell this lovely flower and be nice to all people and animals.
Breath out – send loving thoughts to anyone who is sad.

- Repeat breathing 5-10 times...slow & deep

Other Breathing Suggestions:
- Breathe in while whispering to the count of 5, and exhale while whispering to the count of 5.

Calm Cottontail
Courtesy Lesson Plan

Exercise #3
Calm Cottontail Stretch

- Get comfortable – remove shoes and be on a nonslid surface.

Calm Cottontail is going to show you how you can extend a hand to someone – how you can be nice and courteous to someone who may need your help or your kindness.

Instructions for the stretch:
Sit on both knees. Extend left leg out to the side. Stretch left arm down and stretch to touch your toes. Extend right arm straight up, bending over and feeling the stretch.

- Rest in this pose for 10 seconds to start…then longer.

As you do this stretch, imagine sitting with Calm Cottontail in the middle of the garden…everyone who comes your way, you greet with a nice hello and shake of the hand. Who might come by – do you see any garden animals coming your way?

- Ask the children questions: Who would you like to meet? What would you say to them?

Calm Cottontails
Courtesy Lesson Plan

Exercise #4
Bunny Whisperer

- Sit in a comfortable position.

Calm Cottontail wants to introduce us to his friend, the Firefly.
This amazing beetle is also called a lightning bug or a glowworm.
It flies around on beautiful summer nights...lighting up the night sky.
They are so courteous and nice – letting children catch them and hold them in their hand. Have you ever tried this?

- Show the child a photo of a real Firefly.

- Have children close their eyes.

Calm Cottontail says that you can learn to talk to all of his friends in the Peaceful Garden...that you can become the Bunny Whisperer. All you have to do is keep your eyes closed, imagine walking up to firefly, catching him in your hand, and in a very soft, calm voice talk to him...what would you like to say, do you have any questions for him? You can give him a name...what would you like to call him?

- Practice talking like the Bunny Whisperer... What would you like to talk about today?

Calm Cottontails
Courtesy Lesson Plan

Exercise #5
Bridge of Dreams

- **Sit with legs crossed and eyes closed.**

Calm Cottontail shows you the bridge of dreams…it is here that you can ask for anything. Keep your eyes closed and think about what you want to wish for today….

Before you can walk across the bridge, you must promise to be nice to all those around you…using your manners, being nice at all times. As you begin to walk across the bridge, you see that other people are following you. You begin to talk to them – saying hello and asking them questions. You are no longer lonely – it's a wonderful feeling. On the other side of the bridge is your new, special friend waiting for you – the firefly.

When you get to the other side of the bridge, you all celebrate by dancing in the moonlight – Calm Cottontail loves to dance when he's happy!

- To have some fun, you can dance around the room – it will feel good!

- You can have a <u>Midnight Tea Party</u> – who would you like to invite?

Calm Cottontails
Courtesy Lesson Plan

Exercise #6
Moonbeam Rides

- **Sit with legs crossed and eyes closed.**

The peaceful garden is turning pink...keep your eyes closed and imagine seeing this color all around you. As you look at Calm Cottontail, he is also changing – his cottontail is turning pink – can you see it? This reminds us, that we can also change – we can change how we feel at any moment. Right now, let's open our heart to all people and animals, spreading kindness at all times.

You see a pink moonbeam coming your way – you, Calm Cottontail and firefly all jump on. You are so happy that you can make people feel better...you enjoy using your manners and being nice to people you meet. Helping others makes you not feel lonely or scared. You watch your problems disappear into the night sky...one by one. Close your eyes and watch this...

On the moonbeam is the softest bed of forest moss and beautiful ferns acting as a blanket. You lay your head down and watch the night sky...it's lighting up with all the fireflies...they are all your friends now...they are so proud of how courteous you are to others – using your manners, being nice, opening your heart.

- **You can give the children a pink pompom, so they will remember to take time to listen all day.**

Calm Cottontail
Courtesy Lesson Plan

Exercise #7
Moonlight Serenade

- Sit in a comfortable position.

As the moonbeam goes over the trees, you hear the music of the night – birds singing, crickets chirping – take time to listen. It's like a beautiful Moonlight Serenade.

- It's your turn to sing now:

  "I am courteous...I am courteous."
  Can you hear the birds singing it with you?

You can sing this serenade anytime you are lonely or don't know what to say to someone. By singing this song, you are sending peace out to the whole world.

Bunny Blossoms
Every time you sing this song, it wakes up all of the flowers in the garden. And if you look very closely, you can see them all turning into Bunny Blossoms – they are all taking the shape of little bunnies...and showing you that anything is possible.

- Play a nature CD for relaxation at this time.

Calm Cottontail
Courtesy Lesson Plan

Exercise #8
Landing back in the Enchanted Garden

• Lay down with eye pillow.

You smell the Night Scented Stock flower again – breathe in the beautiful fragrance, breathe out into the night sky.

Sometimes we all feel lonely or alone. At times like this, it's best to try to reach out and help someone else – by helping others, we will feel better.

Let's take a walk in our peaceful garden. As we do, we hear a cry for help. As you look around, you see a tiny baby animal. Close your eyes and imagine what animal it is...can you see it? It looks so helpless and alone. You bend down to pick it up and hold it very close to you. As you do, it begins to stop crying. You stroke its head and talk (in your Bunny Whisperer voice...). What things would you say to make it feel better? As you are talking, the baby's mother comes to you – she is so relieved that you helped her baby. You feel so good inside...and lay your head down to rest.

Calm Cottontail
Courtesy Lesson Plan

Exercise #9
Bunny Hugs

• Have a Calm Cottontail Bunny with you now.

You have been so kind to everyone in the garden today. Calm Cottontail helped you and you're going to give him a big Bunny Hug now.

You might want to give someone else a big Bunny Hug...can you think of anyone?

Exercise #10
Courage

It takes great courage to learn something new...and do something that is very difficult. By doing this lesson, you had great courage and Calm Cottontail and your new friend, firefly are very proud of you!

Do the Courage Stretch – be proud!!!!

Calm Cottontail
Courtesy Lesson Plan

Quick Calming Tips

Lavender Wand
When you wave the lavender wand, children will know it's time to go their peaceful garden and think about being kind to someone.

Bunny Breath Breaths
These can be done anytime, anywhere. Have children close their eyes and imagine that they are breathing in the Night Scented Stock flower.

Calm Cottontail Stretch
Take time to do the Calm Cottontail Courtesy Stretch during the day.

Bunny Whisperer
Remember to take time to be courteous to others today – listen, help, and use your manners. Remember your friend, Firefly.

Bridge of Dreams
Remember to leave your problems behind before you move on.

Moonbeam Rides
Give children a pink pompom to remind them of courtesy during the day.

Moonlight Serenades
Take time to listen to Nature CD and say affirmation throughout the day.
"I am courteous. I am courteous." Look for the Bunny Blossoms.

Calm Cottontail Bunny
Let's be kind to Calm Cottontail today – and all animals.
Hold Calm Cottontail and give him a Bunny Hug.

Courage
Remember to do the courage stretch when you are feeling worried or scared. You can do anything!

Courtesy

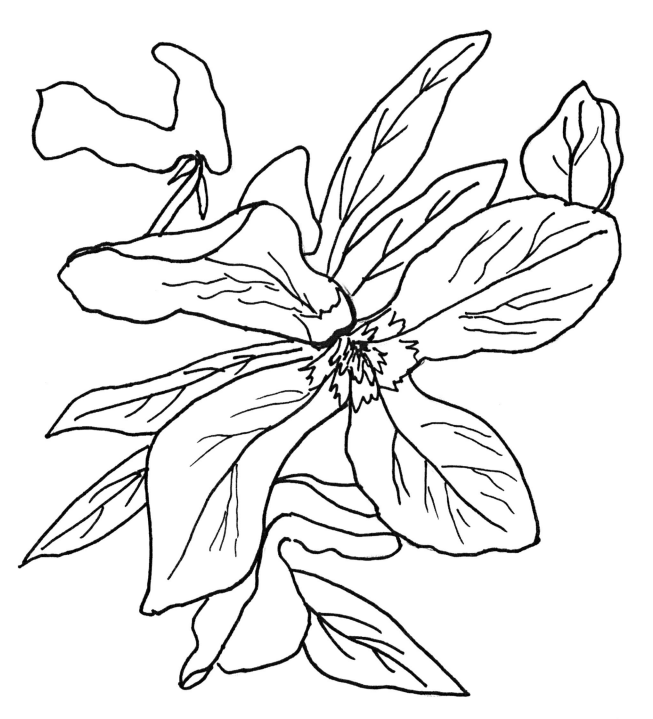

NIGHT SCENTED STOCK

Calm Cottontail
Gratitude Lesson Plan

Exercise #1
Entering the Peaceful Garden

- Sit with legs crossed and eyes closed.
- Use Lavender Wand

We're getting ready to enter our peaceful garden....close your eyes, relax and just sit back. We can think about all the special things in our life – we have so much to be grateful for.

Calm Cottontail is going to meet us in the garden. Rabbits are so grateful for all the wonderful things a garden provides. They get so excited when there's good food to eat, and a safe place to hide, and a quiet place to sit.

Say together:
   "I am going to my peaceful garden where I will take time to be grateful for all the wonderful gifts in my life."

Calm Cottontail
Gratitude Lesson Plan

Exercise #2
Bunny Breath Breaths

- Sit with their legs crossed or on knees.

Calm Cottontail is sitting under the Night Blooming Cereus flower. This is probably the most magnificent flower in the entire garden! It's also called the "Queen of the Night" flower because it only blooms one night out of the entire year!

Calm Cottontail says that people wait all year and plan parties to see the "Queen of the Night" bloom. Make every day a celebration like this – for all the good things in your life.

Breathe in – I take time to see all the good things in my life.
Breath out – I say "thank you" for everything that I have.

- Repeat breathing 5-10 times…slow & deep

Other Breathing Suggestions:
- Each time, you take a breath – think of something good in your life.
- See how many things you can think of – make a list!

Calm Cottontail
Gratitude Lesson Plan

Exercise #3
Calm Cottontail Stretch

- Get comfortable – remove shoes and be on a nonslid surface.

Calm Cottontail is going to show you how you can take time to be grateful for all the good things in your life.

Instructions for the stretch:
Sit on the ground. Have both legs stretched out in front of you with your back straight. Bend right leg inward, placing heel against your thigh. Keep the left leg straight out in front of you. Stretch arms above head and then bend all the way down to your foot. Then switch sides. Then you can place both legs straight out. Stretch arms above head and then bend them all the way down to your feet.

- Rest in this pose for 10 seconds to start...then longer.

As you do this stretch, imagine sitting with Calm Cottontail in the middle of your garden. You look around and see so many wonderful things to be happy and grateful for. Anytime you are feeling sad or upset, just look around your life to see all the gifts that are around – you have so much.

Calm Cottontails
Gratitude Lesson Plan

Exercise #4
Bunny Whisperer

- Sit in a comfortable position.

Calm Cottontail wants to introduce you to his friend, the Ladybug. People get so excited when they find a ladybug, or one lands on their hand – it's supposed to bring good luck. Ladybugs are actually beetles and they come in many different colors – red, pink, yellow, white and even blue! Imagine if a ladybug landed on you right now – you would be very grateful for your good luck!

- Show the child a photo of a real Ladybug.

- Have children close their eyes.

Calm Cottontail says that you can learn to talk to all of his friends in the Peaceful Garden...that you can become the Bunny Whisperer. All you have to do is keep your eyes closed, imagine walking up to the Ladybug. What would you like to ask him? Take a long look at him – what would you like to name him?

- Practice talking like the Bunny Whisperer... What would you like to talk about today?

- Remember to make a wish on your Ladybug today!

Calm Cottontails
Gratitude Lesson Plan

Exercise #5
Bridge of Dreams

- **Sit with legs crossed and eyes closed.**

Calm Cottontail shows you the bridge of dreams...it is here that you can ask for anything. Keep your eyes closed and think about what you want to wish for today....

Before you can walk across the bridge, you must promise to be grateful for all the gifts in your life – not take anything for granted, but appreciate and be happy for all that you have. You new friend, Ladybug is flying next to you.

When you get to the other side of the bridge, you all celebrate by dancing in the moonlight – Calm Cottontail loves to dance when he's happy! Kick up those big feet and jump all around!

- To have some fun, you can dance around the room – it will feel good!

- You can also have a <u>Midnight Tea Party</u> – who would you invite?

Calm Cottontails
Gratitude Lesson Plan

Exercise #6
Moonbeam Rides

- **Sit with legs crossed and eyes closed.**

The peaceful garden is turning orange…keep your eyes closed and imagine seeing this color all around you. As you look at Calm Cottontail, he is also changing – his cottontail is turning orange – can you see it? This reminds us, that we can also change – we can change how we feel at any moment. Right now, let's be grateful for all the gifts in our life – we have so much.

You see an orange moonbeam coming your way – you, Calm Cottontail and Ladybug all jump on. The next time you are feeling sad or upset, just look around and see all the good things in your life – all your gifts. You watch your problems disappear into the night sky…one by one. Close your eyes and watch this…

On the moonbeam is the softest bed of forest moss and beautiful ferns acting as a blanket. You lay your head down and Ladybug lands on the Queen of the Night Flower next to…you both feel very peaceful at this moment.

- **You can give the children an orange pompom, so they will remember to accept whatever comes.**

Calm Cottontail
Gratitude Lesson Plan

Exercise #7
Moonlight Serenade

- Sit in a comfortable position.

As the moonbeam goes over the trees, you hear the music of the night – birds singing, crickets chirping – take time to listen. It's like a beautiful Moonlight Serenade.

- It's your turn to sing now:

  "I am grateful." "I am grateful."
  Can you hear the birds singing it with you?

By singing this song, you are sending these good thoughts of gratitude out to the world.

Bunny Blossoms
Every time you sing this song, it wakes up all the flowers in the garden. And if you look very closely, you can see them all turning into Bunny Blossoms – they are all taking the shape of little bunnies...and showing you that anything is possible!

- Play a nature CD for relaxation at this time.

Calm Cottontail
Gratitude Lesson Plan

Exercise #8
Landing back in the Enchanted Garden

- Lay down with eye pillow.

You smell the Queen of the Night flower again – breathe in the beautiful fragrance, breathe out into the night sky.

Sometimes we are sad and disappointed and don't see all the good things in our life. We must remember to always take time to be grateful.

Let's take a walk in our peaceful garden. You find the perfect spot to sit and rest. You close your eyes and begin thinking about all the important things in your life. As you do, you suddenly find yourself floating down a beautiful pond. All around you are lighted candles, which are lighting the way. As each candle floats by you, it reminds you of something special in your life. As you watch one candle after another move by you, you begin to see how many things you have to be grateful for. Now whenever you are wanting more, just look around at all the candles in your life and say a big "thank you" for everything you have!

Calm Cottontail
Gratitude Lesson Plan

Exercise #9
Bunny Hugs

• Have a Calm Cottontail Bunny with you now.

You have so much to be grateful for – so many gifts in your life. Calm Cottontail helped you and you're going to give him a big Bunny Hug now.

You might want to give someone else a big Bunny Hug…can you think of anyone?

Exercise #10
Courage

It takes great courage to learn something new…and do something that is very difficult. By doing this lesson, you had great courage and Calm Cottontail and your new friend, Ladybug are very proud of you!

Do the Courage Stretch – be proud!!!!

Calm Cottontail
Gratitude Lesson Plan

Quick Calming Tips

Lavender Wand
When you wave the lavender wand, children will know it's time to be grateful for all the wonderful gifts in your life.

Bunny Breath Breaths
These can be done anytime, anywhere. Have children close their eyes and imagine that they are breathing in the Night Blooming Cereus or "Queen of the Night" flower.

Calm Cottontail Stretch
Take time to do the Calm Cottontail Gratitude Stretch during the day.

Bunny Whisperer
Remember to be grateful today. Think of your friend, the Ladybug.

Bridge of Dreams
Remember to leave your problems behind before you move on.

Moonbeam Rides
Give children an orange pompom to remind them of being grateful today.

Moonlight Serenades
Take time to listen to Nature CD and say your affirmation throughout the day. "I am grateful." Remember to always look for the Bunny Blossoms.

Calm Cottontail Bunny
Let's sit with Calm Cottontail – we both will be grateful.
Hold Calm Cottontail and give him a Bunny Hug.

Courage
Take time to do the courage stretch whenever you are feeling worried or scared. Remember you can do anything!

Gratitude

NIGHT BLOOMING CEREUS

Calm Cottontail
Listening Lesson Plan

Exercise #1
Entering the Peaceful Garden

- Sit with legs crossed and eyes closed.
- Use Lavender Wand

We're getting ready to enter our peaceful garden....close your eyes, relax and bring peace into your heart. As we do this, we're going to listen very carefully to all the sounds around us...what do you hear?

Calm Cottontail is going to meet us in the garden. Do you know that he listens very well. His big ears help him to hear many things...even things far away. He likes to sit very still in the garden and listen to all the sounds around him. Let's be like Calm Cottontail and sit very quietly and just listen...after we do this for a while, he will appear to us.

- Play a game: See how long you can sit and just listen – time yourself and then increase it each time you do this lesson.

- Say together:
  "I am going to my peaceful garden where I will listen very carefully."

Calm Cottontail
Listening Lesson Plan

Exercise #2
Bunny Breath Breaths

* Sit with their legs crossed or on knees.

Calm Cottontail is sitting under the Night Blooming Jasmine flower. This flower grows in Asia. It grows very tall – up to 12 feet high! It has very small, delicate flowers stretching as high as they can go.

Calm Cottontail keeps his nose moving and twitching at all times to take in big breaths, so he will be happy in the garden. Let's be like Calm Cottontail and breathe...

Breath in – smell this lovely flower and take time to listen.
Breath out – I hear wonderful things all around me.

* Repeat breathing 5-10 times...slow & deep

Other Breathing Suggestions:
- Breathe in while whispering to the count of 5, and exhale while whispering to the count of 5.

Calm Cottontail
Listening Lesson Plan

Exercise #3
Calm Cottontail Stretch

- Get comfortable – remove shoes and be on a nonslid surface.

Calm Cottontail is going to show you how he listens in the garden.

Instructions for the stretch:
Sit in crossed-legged position. Bend to right side, extending arm and resting elbow on the ground. Bend left arm up to cup ear. Then switch sides.

- Rest in this pose for 10 seconds to start…then longer.

As you do this stretch, imagine sitting with Calm Cottontail in the middle of the garden…the two of you are so still and are listening so carefully.

- Ask the children questions: What sounds do you hear in the garden? What is your favorite sound?

Calm Cottontails
Listening Lesson Plan

Exercise #4
Bunny Whisperer

• **Sit in a comfortable position.**

Calm Cottontail wants to introduce us to his friend, the Nightingale bird.
This bird is called the "Night Songstress" because the male nightingale bird sings such pretty songs all night long. For such a small bird, it can produce large, beautiful sounds.

• Show the child a photo of a real Nightengale bird.

• Have children close their eyes.

Calm Cottontail says that you can learn to talk to all of his friends in the Peaceful Garden...that you can become the Bunny Whisperer. All you have to do is keep your eyes closed, imagine walking up to the Nightengale bird, and in a very soft, calm voice talk to him...what would you like to say, do you have any questions for him? You can give him a name...what would you like to call him?

• Practice talking like the Bunny Whisperer... What would you like to talk about today?

Calm Cottontails
Listening Lesson Plan

Exercise #5
Bridge of Dreams

- **Sit with legs crossed and eyes closed.**

Calm Cottontail shows you the bridge of dreams…it is here that you can ask for anything. Keep your eyes closed and think about what you want to wish for today….

Before you can walk across the bridge, you must promise to try to listen more…listen to the people and sounds around you. As you begin to walk across the bridge, you hear beautiful sounds in the garden – sounds you never heard before…everything is sounding so lovely. On the other side of the bridge is your new, special friend waiting for you – the Nightengale bird.

 When you get to the other side of the bridge, you all celebrate by dancing in the moonlight – Calm Cottontail loves to dance when he's happy!

- To have some fun, you can dance around the room – it will feel good!

- You can also have a <u>Midnight Tea Party</u> – who would you like to invite?

Calm Cottontails
Listening Lesson Plan

Exercise #6
Moonbeam Rides

- **Sit with legs crossed and eyes closed.**

The peaceful garden is turning green…keep your eyes closed and imagine seeing this color all around you. As you look at Calm Cottontail, he is also changing – his cottontail is turning green – can you see it? This reminds us, that we can also change – we can change how we feel at any moment. Right now, let's open our heart and our ears and listen to all the sounds around us.

You see a green moonbeam coming your way – you, Calm Cottontail and Nightengale all jump on. You are able to pay attention and hear all the sounds around you – it's so amazing! You watch your problems disappear into the night sky…one by one. Close your eyes and watch this…

On the moonbeam is the softest bed of forest moss and beautiful ferns acting as a blanket. You lay your head down, everything is so quiet, you can hear a Luna Moth's wings going by you…it sounds so wonderful!

- **You can give the children a green pompom, so they will remember to take time to listen all day.**

Calm Cottontail
Listening Lesson Plan

Exercise #7
Moonlight Serenade

- **Sit in a comfortable position.**

As the moonbeam goes over the trees, you hear the music of the night – birds singing, crickets chirping – take time to listen. It's like a beautiful Moonlight Serenade.

- It's your turn to sing now:

    "I am listening, I am listening…"
    Can you hear the birds singing it with you?

You can sing this serenade anytime you are having a difficult time paying attention or listening. By singing this song, you are sending peace out to the whole world.

Bunny Blossoms
Every time you sing this song, it wakes up all the flowers in the garden. And if you look very closely, you can see them all turning into Bunny Blossoms – they are all taking the shape of little bunnies…and showing you that anything is possible!

- Play a nature CD for relaxation at this time.

Calm Cottontail
Listening Lesson Plan

Exercise #8
Landing back in the Enchanted Garden

- Lay down with eye pillow.

You smell the Night Blooming Jasmine flower again – breathe in the beautiful fragrance, breathe out into the night sky. You are tired and lay your head down. You start thinking, sometimes it's hard to pay attention and listen to people. You know that you can be like Calm Cottontail and listen very well...these thoughts go through your mind as you float away on the moonbeam. You feel the soft touch of Calm Cottontail as he lays down next to you. He loves to be close to you. You hear a beautiful sound...as you listen more carefully, you realize it's a hummingbird's wings – it's getting a drink from a flower and you can hear it. The sound is so amazing. The next time you're having difficulty listening play a game called "echo," you will repeat back what you heard three times – once you have done this, think of hearing the hummingbird's wings and you will be able to listen and remember. Your garden friends will help you.

Calm Cottontail
Listening Lesson Plan

Exercise #9
Bunny Hugs

- Have a Calm Cottontail Bunny with you now.

All the beautiful sounds are filling your heart with love and happiness.
Calm Cottontail helped you and you're going to give him a big Bunny Hug now.

You might want to give someone else a big Bunny Hug...can you think of anyone?

Exercise #10
Courage

It takes great courage to learn something new...and do something that is very difficult. By doing this lesson, you had great courage and Calm Cottontail and your new friend, Nightengale bird are very proud of you!

Do the Courage Stretch – be proud!!!!

Calm Cottontail
Listening Lesson Plan

Quick Calming Tips

Lavender Wand
When you wave the lavender wand, children will know it's time to go to their peaceful garden and listen to all the sounds.

Bunny Breath Breaths
These can be done anytime, anywhere. Have children close their eyes and imagine that they are breathing in the Night Blooming Jasmine flower.

Calm Cottontail Stretch
Take time to do the Calm Cottontail Listening Stretch during the day.

Bunny Whisperer
 Remember to listen to all those around you today. Remember your friend, Nightingale bird.

Bridge of Dreams
Remember to leave your problems behind before you move on.

Moonbeam Rides
Give children a green pompom to remind them of listening during the day.

Moonlight Serenades
Take time to listen to Nature CD and say affirmation throughout the day. "I am listening. I am listening." Remember to look for the Bunny Blossoms.

Calm Cottontail Bunny
Let's think about what Calm Cottontail might be saying to us right now? Hold Calm Cottontail and give him a Bunny Hug.

Courage
Take time to do the courage stretch whenever you are feeling worried or scared. Remember you can do anything!

Listening

NIGHT BLOOMING JASMINE

Calm Cottontail
Love Lesson Plan

Exercise #1
Entering the Peaceful Garden

- Sit with legs crossed and eyes closed.
- Use Lavender Wand

We're getting ready to enter our peaceful garden....close your eyes, relax and bring loving thoughts into your heart.

Calm Cottontail is going to meet us in the garden. People all around the world just love rabbits. When they see a cute rabbit, it brings good feelings to their heart and they immediately want to touch, pet and hold the adorable rabbit. When we look at Calm Cottontail, we think loving thoughts right away.

- Say together:
  "I am going to my peaceful garden where I will find loving thoughts and bring them into my heart."

Calm Cottontail
Love Lesson Plan

Exercise #2
Bunny Breath Breaths

• Sit with their legs crossed or on knees.

Calm Cottontail is sitting under the Moonflower. This flower has huge leaves – it's the biggest flower in the garden! And they have one other amazing quality – their leaves are heart shaped!

Calm Cottontail says holding this heart shaped flower and breathing always reminds him of loving thoughts.

Breath in – smelling this heart shaped flower, I feel love.
Breath out – I send this love out to the world for all to share.

• Repeat breathing 5-10 times…slow & deep

Other Breathing Suggestions:
- Each time we breath in, we think of someone that we love…
- Each time we breathe out, we send love to this person…

Calm Cottontail
Love Lesson Plan

Exercise #3
Calm Cottontail Stretch

- Get comfortable – remove shoes and be on a nonslid surface.

Calm Cottontail is going to show you how you to bring love to your heart – this will always make you feel good inside.

Instructions for the stretch:

Sit on the ground with your legs in a crossed position. Sit with back straight. Place hands by your heart. Sit in this position for as long as you can.
You can also raise your arms straight up, gazing upward. You can flow up and down with your arms.

- Rest in this pose for 10 seconds to start…then longer.

As you do this stretch, imagine sitting with Calm Cottontail in the middle of the garden. He looks so calm and peaceful and you love him so much. The moon is shining so brightly tonight, that it looks like it's wrapping around Calm Cottontail in a warm embrace – giving him a big hug. You sit down next to him, and feel the moon's warm embrace around you…you feel very loved at this moment.

- Think about someone that you love. Send love out to them right now.

Calm Cottontails
Love Lesson Plan

Exercise #4
Bunny Whisperer

- Sit in a comfortable position.

Calm Cottontail wants to introduce us to his friend, the Barn Owl. This is an amazing bird that has huge wings and soft feathers that are almost silent as they fly. They also have a heart-shaped face!

- Show the child a photo of a Barn Owl.

- Have children close their eyes.

Calm Cottontail says that you can learn to talk to all of his friends in the Peaceful Garden…that you can become the Bunny Whisperer. All you have to do is keep your eyes closed, imagine walking up to Barn Owl. What would you like to ask him? Take a long look at him – what would you like to name him?

- Practice talking like the Bunny Whisperer… What would you like to talk about today?

Calm Cottontails
Love Lesson Plan

Exercise #5
Bridge of Dreams

- Sit with legs crossed and eyes closed.

Calm Cottontail shows you the bridge of dreams...it is here that you can ask for anything. Keep your eyes closed and think about what you want to wish for today....

Before you can walk across the bridge, you must think about something you love – bring that thought to your mind. Remember to always love yourself – you're very special. As you begin to walk across the bridge, you feel wonderful inside and so happy. As you walk across the bridge, your new friend, Barn Own is flying next to you and as you look at his heart-shaped face, you feel love.

When you get to the other side of the bridge, you all celebrate by dancing in the moonlight – Calm Cottontail loves to dance when he's happy!

- To have some fun, you can dance around the room – it will feel good!

- You can also have a <u>Midnight Tea Party</u> – who would you invite?

Calm Cottontails
Love Lesson Plan

Exercise #6
Moonbeam Rides

- **Sit with legs crossed and eyes closed.**

The peaceful garden is turning red…keep your eyes closed and imagine seeing this color all around you. As you look at Calm Cottontail, he is also changing – his cottontail is turning red – can you see it? This reminds us, that we can also change – we can change how we feel at any moment. Right now, let's open our heart to love…there are so many people in our lives that we can love.

You see a red moonbeam coming your way – you, Calm Cottontail and Barn Owl all jump on. You are so happy that you can find love all around. The next time you are feeling alone or sad, you will think of this. You watch your problems disappear into the night sky…one by one. Close your eyes and watch this…

On the moonbeam is the softest bed of forest moss and beautiful ferns acting as a blanket. You lay your head down and look up into the sky, and you start thinking about someone you love. You imagine that you are walking through your peaceful garden and picking the most beautiful bouquet of flowers for this special person…think about what they would like. Now imagine yourself giving love…and giving your bouquet to this person. How does it feel?

- **You can give the children a red pompom, so they will remember to be loving all day long.**

Calm Cottontail
Love Lesson Plan

Exercise #7
Moonlight Serenade

- Sit in a comfortable position.

As the moonbeam goes over the trees, you hear the music of the night – birds singing, crickets chirping – take time to listen. It's like a beautiful Moonlight Serenade.

- It's your turn to sing now:

   "I am love. I am love."
   Can you hear the birds singing it with you?

You can sing this serenade anytime you are lonely or feeling sad. By singing this song, you are sending love out to the whole world.

Bunny Blossoms:
Every time you sing this song, it wakes up all the flowers in the garden. And if you look very closely, you can see them all turning into Bunny Blossoms – they are all taking the shape of little bunnies...and showing you that anything is possible!

- Play a nature CD for relaxation at this time.

Calm Cottontail
Love Lesson Plan

Exercise #8
Landing back in the Enchanted Garden

• Lay down with eye pillow.

You smell the Moonflower flower again – breathe in the beautiful fragrance, breathe out into the night sky.

Sometimes we feel alone or sad. We know we can make these feelings drift away, by bringing loving thoughts into our hearts.

Let's take a walk in our peaceful garden. You're feeling a little sleepy, so you look for a soft, comfy spot to rest your head. As you lay down, you feel someone lay a blanket on you. As you look more closely, you realize it's a red cape. As soon as they lay it on you, you feel warmth and comfort – almost like it's glowing. It feels like a giant hug and you can fill the love all around you. As you look at this glowing red cape, you realize that it has different patches on it – and each patch is someone or something that you love - it's amazing! Remember that anytime you are feeling lonely or sad, you can put on your "Cape of Comfort" and let the love warm you.

<u>Calm Cottontail</u>
Love Lesson Plan

<u>Exercise #9</u>
Bunny Hugs

• Have a Calm Cottontail Bunny with you now.

You have so much love in your heart right now. Calm Cottontail helped you and you're going to give him a big Bunny Hug now.

You might want to give someone else a big Bunny Hug…can you think of anyone?

<u>Exercise #10</u>
Courage

It takes great courage to learn something new…and do something that is very difficult. By doing this lesson, you had great courage and Calm Cottontail and your new friend, Barn Owl are very proud of you!

Do the Courage Stretch – be proud!!!!

Calm Cottontail
Love Lesson Plan

Quick Calming Tips

Lavender Wand
When you wave the lavender wand, children will know it's time to go their peaceful garden and think loving thoughts.

Bunny Breath Breaths
These can be done anytime, anywhere. Have children close their eyes and imagine that they are breathing in the Moonflower flower.

Calm Cottontail Stretch
Take time to do the Calm Cottontail Love Stretch during the day.

Bunny Whisperer
Remember to take time to spread love to others today. Think of your friend, Barn Owl.

Bridge of Dreams
Remember to leave your problems behind before you move on.

Moonbeam Rides
Give children a red pompom to remind them of love during the day.

Moonlight Serenades
Take time to listen to Nature CD and say affirmation throughout the day.
"I am love. I am love." Remember to look for the Bunny Blossoms.

Calm Cottontail Bunny
Let's send love to Calm Cottontail...his heart is lighting up now.
Hold Calm Cottontail and give him a Bunny Hug.

Courage
Take time to do the courage stretch whenever you are feeling worried or scared. Remember you can do anything!

Love

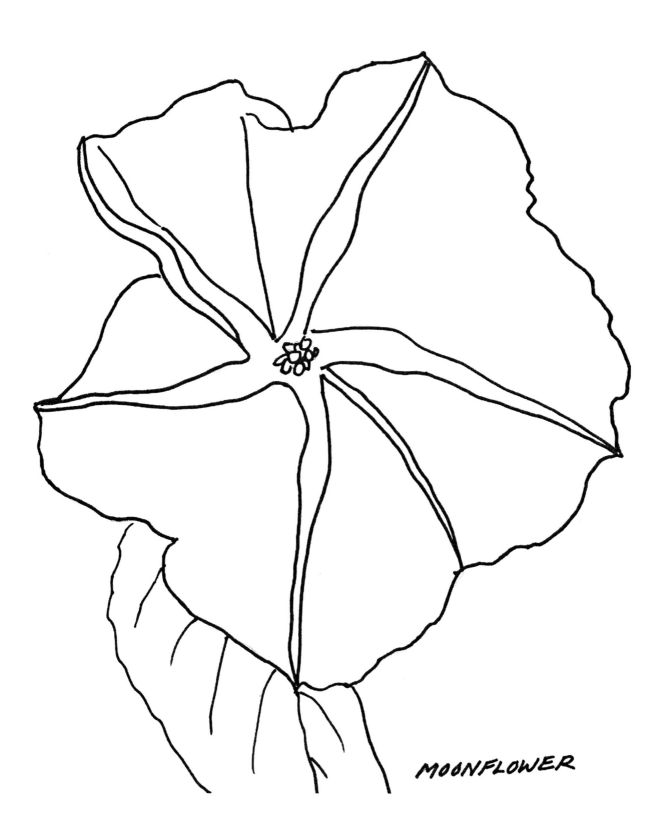

MOONFLOWER

Calm Cottontail
Patience Lesson Plan

Exercise #1
Entering the Peaceful Garden

- Sit with legs crossed and eyes closed.
- Use Lavender Wand

We're getting ready to enter our peaceful garden....close your eyes, relax and just sit back...it may take us awhile to get there today, so we must try to be patient.

Calm Cottontail is going to meet us in the garden. Rabbits have the wonderful ability to be very patient. They can sit in the middle of the garden for a very long time...just waiting, being very still. We can learn a lot from them – by just watching and doing what they do.

Say together:
   "I am going to my peaceful garden where I will be patient."

Calm Cottontail
Patience Lesson Plan

Exercise #2
Bunny Breath Breaths

- Sit with their legs crossed or on knees.

Calm Cottontail is sitting under the Four O'Clock flower. This amazing flower grows in Peru. It's a very interesting flower because it can change color...if you watch very carefully a yellow flower can turn pink and a white flower can turn violet. Sometimes there are different color flowers on the same branch. Long-tongued moths love this flower.

Calm Cottontail says by doing your breathing, you can practice having patience.

Breath in – smelling this flower, I slow down and wait.
Breath out – I choose to be patient at this time.

- Repeat breathing 5-10 times...slow & deep

Other Breathing Suggestions:
- As children breath in, have them imagine the flower being one color...
- As children breath out, have the flower change color...picture these colors in our minds.
- Have children think of times when they must be patient –
  then have them try their Bunny Breath Breaths during this time.

Calm Cottontail
Patience Lesson Plan

Exercise #3
Calm Cottontail Stretch

- Get comfortable – remove shoes and be on a nonslid surface.

Calm Cottontail is going to show you how to take time to work on your thoughts.

Instructions for the stretch:

Stand straight. Then bend knees, keeping back straight. Extend arms straight out in front, squatting while holding this stretch. See how long you can stay like this – have patience.

You can practice going lower...how low can you go?

- Rest in this pose for 10 seconds to start...then longer.

As you do this stretch, imagine sitting with Calm Cottontail in the middle of your peaceful garden. You both are really looking forward to your friends coming, but right now, you are having patience and just sitting, waiting. As you do, you are enjoying the quiet time – and you feel so peaceful and calm.

Calm Cottontails
Patience Lesson Plan

Exercise #4
Bunny Whisperer

- Sit in a comfortable position.

Calm Cottontail wants to introduce you to his friend, the Hummingbird Moth. This is an amazing creature – it's a moth, but it looks like a Hummingbird! It can move so fast, but when it needs to eat, it slows down and has patience while it waits on a flower.

- Show the child a photo of a real Hummingbird Moth.

- Have children close their eyes.

Calm Cottontail says that you can learn to talk to all of his friends in the Peaceful Garden…that you can become the Bunny Whisperer. All you have to do is keep your eyes closed, imagine walking up to the Hummingbird Moth. What would you like to ask him? Take a long look at him – what would you like to name him?

- Practice talking like the Bunny Whisperer… What would you like to talk about today?

Calm Cottontails
Patience Lesson Plan

Exercise #5
Bridge of Dreams

- Sit with legs crossed and eyes closed.

Calm Cottontail shows you the bridge of dreams...it is here that you can ask for anything. Keep your eyes closed and think about what you want to wish for today....

Before you can walk across the bridge, you must promise to walk slowly and have patience about getting to the other side...you even stop to help an animal across on your way – there is no hurry. You new friend, Hummingbird Moth is flying next to you.

When you get to the other side of the bridge, you all celebrate by dancing in the moonlight – Calm Cottontail loves to dance when he's happy! Kick up those big feet and jump all around!

- To have some fun, you can dance around the room – it will feel good!

- You can also have a Midnight Tea Party – who would you invite?

Calm Cottontails
Patience Lesson Plan

Exercise #6
Moonbeam Rides

- **Sit with legs crossed and eyes closed.**

The peaceful garden is turning white...keep your eyes closed and imagine seeing this color all around you. As you look at Calm Cottontail, he is also changing – his cottontail is turning white – can you see it? This reminds us, that we can also change – we can change how we feel at any moment. Right now, let's open our mind to patience...knowing we can wait for things.

You see a white moonbeam coming your way – you, Calm Cottontail and Hummingbird Moth all jump on. The next time you are feeling anxious or in a hurry, just remember that you can change your actions...you can slow down and go with patience. You watch your problems disappear into the night sky...one by one. Close your eyes and watch this...

On the moonbeam is the softest bed of forest moss and beautiful ferns acting as a blanket. You lay your head down and hear the wings of the Hummingbird Moth next to you. He is taking a rest on the Four O' Clock Flower and just resting next to you...you both feel very peaceful at this moment.

- **You can give the children a white pompom, so they will remember to take time to listen all day.**

Calm Cottontail
Patience Lesson Plan

Exercise #7
Moonlight Serenade

- Sit in a comfortable position.

As the moonbeam goes over the trees, you hear the music of the night – birds singing, crickets chirping – take time to listen. It's like a beautiful Moonlight Serenade.

- It's your turn to sing now:

  "I am patient.   I am patient."
   Can you hear the birds singing it with you?

You can sing this serenade anytime you are lonely or don't know what to say to someone. By singing this song, you are sending peace out to the whole world.

Bunny Blossoms
Every time you sing this song, it wakes up all of the flowers in the garden. And if you look very closely, you can see them all turning into Bunny Blossoms – they are all taking the shape of little bunnies...and showing you that anything is possible!

- Play a nature CD for relaxation at this time.

Calm Cottontail
Patience Lesson Plan

Exercise #8
Landing back in the Enchanted Garden

• Lay down with eye pillow.

You smell the Four O'Clock flower again – breathe in the beautiful fragrance, breathe out into the night sky.

Sometimes we are in hurry or feeling anxious. We know we can make these feelings drift away, by bringing patience into our hearts.

Let's take a walk in our peaceful garden. It's a beautiful evening out, the moon is shining bright and the wind is blowing slightly. As you look around, you see a friend way across the garden…they are standing in a thick part of the garden. The only way to reach them is by putting down stepping stones, so that you can create a path to them. This will take some time, but you know that you can be patient and work hard to create your stepping stone path. One by one, you put down the stones, and before you know it, you reach your friend! You both sit together under the Faraway Tree and talk for a very long time.

Calm Cottontail
Patience Lesson Plan

Exercise #9
Bunny Hugs

• Have a Calm Cottontail Bunny with you now.

It felt good to wait and have patience today. Calm Cottontail helped you and you're going to give him a big Bunny Hug now.

You might want to give someone else a big Bunny Hug...can you think of anyone?

Exercise #10
Courage

It takes great courage to learn something new...and do something that is very difficult. By doing this lesson, you had great courage and Calm Cottontail and your new friend, Hummingbird Moth are very proud of you!

Do the Courage Stretch – be proud!!!!

Calm Cottontail
Patience Lesson Plan

Quick Calming Tips

Lavender Wand
When you wave the lavender wand, children will know it's time to be patient.

Bunny Breath Breaths
These can be done anytime, anywhere. Have children close their eyes and imagine that they are breathing in the Four O' Clock flower.

Calm Cottontail Stretch
Take time to do the Calm Cottontail Patience Stretch during the day.

Bunny Whisperer
Remember to take time to be patient today. Think of your friend, the Hummingbird Moth.

Bridge of Dreams
Remember to leave your problems behind before you move on.

Moonbeam Rides
Give children a white pompom to remind them to be patient today.

Moonlight Serenades
Take time to listen to Nature CD and say your affirmation throughout the day. "I am patient. I am patient." Remember to look for the Bunny Blossoms.

Calm Cottontail Bunny
Let's sit with Calm Cottontail – we both will be patient.
Hold Calm Cottontail and give him a Bunny Hug.

Courage
Take time to do the courage stretch whenever you are feeling worried or scared. Remember you can do anything!

Patience

FOUR O'CLOCK

Calm Cottontail
Peace Lesson Plan

Exercise #1
Entering the Peaceful Garden

- Sit with legs crossed and eyes closed.
- Use Lavender Wand

We're getting ready to enter our peaceful garden….close your eyes, relax and bring peaceful thoughts into your mind.

Calm Cottontail is going to meet us in the garden. Rabbits are one of the most peaceful animals…they can sit for long periods of time without moving. Calm Cottontail says he loves to sit in the garden where it is quiet and beautiful…doing this brings him peace and helps him to relax and not have to move or do anything.

- Say together:
  "I am going to my peaceful garden where I will find peace and bring it into my heart."

Calm Cottontail
Peace Lesson Plan

Exercise #2
Bunny Breath Breaths

• **Sit with their legs crossed or on knees.**

Calm Cottontail is sitting under the Garden Heliotrope flower. This is a very small flower that grows pretty lavender flowers. It grows all summer long and into the fall – it lasts for a very long time. Some people think this flower smells like fresh baked cookies! Yummy – this flower will be very fun to smell!

Calm Cottontail says breathing makes him feel peaceful and calm – that's why he does it all the time!

Breath in – smell this lovely flower and bring peaceful feelings into your heart. Breath out – send peace out to the world.

• Repeat breathing 5-10 times…slow & deep

Other Breathing Suggestions:
- We can feel peaceful at any time during the day by doing our Bunny Breath Breaths – practice this many times throughout the day.

Calm Cottontail
Peace Lesson Plan

Exercise #3
Calm Cottontail Stretch

- Get comfortable – remove shoes and be on a nonslid surface.

Calm Cottontail is going to show you how you can sit and be peaceful – you can do this anytime – just stop, listen and relax.

Instructions for the stretch:
+
Sit on the ground with your legs in a crossed position. Sit with your back straight and tall. Place one leg on top of the other. Place hands on your knees, close eyes and relax. If you are able, you can try placing the other leg on top – if this is uncomfortable, just place one leg.

- Rest in this pose for 10 seconds to start…then longer.

As you do this stretch, imagine sitting with Calm Cottontail in the middle of the garden. You don't need to think of anything – just let happy thoughts float through your mind. You feel so relaxed and peaceful – you could sit here all day.

- How long can you sit like this? Practice each day and see!

Calm Cottontails
Peace Lesson Plan

Exercise #4
Bunny Whisperer

- Sit in a comfortable position.

Calm Cottontail wants to introduce us to his friend, the Luna Moth. This is such an amazing creature! This is one of the largest moths with a giant wingspan.

- Show the child a photo of a real Luna Moth.

- Have children close their eyes.

Calm Cottontail says that you can learn to talk to all of his friends in the Peaceful Garden...that you can become the Bunny Whisperer. All you have to do is keep your eyes closed, imagine walking up to Luna Moth. What would you like to ask him? Take a long look at him – what would you like to name him?

- Practice talking like the Bunny Whisperer... What would you like to talk about today?

Calm Cottontails
Peace Lesson Plan

Exercise #5
Bridge of Dreams

- **Sit with legs crossed and eyes closed.**

Calm Cottontail shows you the bridge of dreams…it is here that you can ask for anything. Keep your eyes closed and think about what you want to wish for today….

Before you can walk across the bridge, you must promise to practice being calm and peaceful each day. As you begin to walk across the bridge, you are feeling so peaceful – it's so quiet here and you have no worries. As you walk across the bridge, your new friend, Luna Moth is flying next to you.

When you get to the other side of the bridge, you all celebrate by dancing in the moonlight – Calm Cottontail loves to dance when he's happy!

- To have some fun, you can dance around the room – it will feel good!

- You can also have a <u>Midnight Tea Party</u> – who would you invite?

Calm Cottontails
Peace Lesson Plan

Exercise #6
Moonbeam Rides

- Sit with legs crossed and eyes closed.

The peaceful garden is turning light blue…keep your eyes closed and imagine seeing this color all around you. As you look at Calm Cottontail, he is also changing – his cottontail is turning light blue – can you see it? This reminds us, that we can also change – we can change how we feel at any moment. Right now, let's open our heart to peace…we can feel peaceful at any time when we think these thoughts.

You see a light blue moonbeam coming your way – you, Calm Cottontail and Luna Moth all jump on. You are so happy that you can find peace at any time. The next time you are feeling worried or anxious, you will know what to do. You watch your problems disappear into the night sky…one by one. Close your eyes and watch this…

On the moonbeam is the softest bed of forest moss and beautiful ferns acting as a blanket. You lay your head down and look up into the sky, you see a whole family of Luna Moths flying over your head…they are so graceful and peaceful in the night sky. As you watch them, you are feeling more relaxed and at peace…you love feeling calm like this and think you will float off to sleep.

- You can give the children a light blue pompom, so they will remember to take time to listen all day.

Calm Cottontail
Peace Lesson Plan

Exercise #7
Moonlight Serenade

- Sit in a comfortable position.

As the moonbeam goes over the trees, you hear the music of the night – birds singing, crickets chirping – take time to listen. It's like a beautiful Moonlight Serenade.

- It's your turn to sing now:

  "I am peace. I am peace."
  Can you hear the birds singing it with you?

You can sing this serenade anytime you are lonely or don't know what to say to someone. By singing this song, you are sending peace out to the whole world.

Bunny Blossoms
Every time you sing this song, it wakes up all the flowers in the garden. And if you look very closely, you can see them all turning into Bunny Blossoms – they are all taking the shape of little bunnies...and showing you that anything is possible!

- Play a nature CD for relaxation at this time.

Calm Cottontail
Peace Lesson Plan

Exercise #8
Landing back in the Enchanted Garden

- Lay down with eye pillow.

You smell the Garden Heliotrope flower again – breathe in the beautiful fragrance, breathe out into the night sky.

Sometimes we feel worried or anxious. We know we can make these feelings drift away, by bringing peace into our hearts.

Let's take a walk in our peaceful garden. You find a very quiet spot and lay your head down. As you drift off to sleep, you imagine a magical pond. You see a lily pad in the middle of this peaceful pond. You imagine yourself sitting on this lily pad – there is no one around and you can only hear the sound of crickets and an occasional frog croaking…can you hear them? As you float away on this lily pad, all of your worries start drifting away in the pond, one by one, they are floating away. You begin to feel so light and happy and peaceful.

Calm Cottontail
Peace Lesson Plan

Exercise #9
Bunny Hugs

- Have a Calm Cottontail Bunny with you now.

You have peace in your heart...you are feeling calm and happy. Calm Cottontail helped you and you're going to give him a big Bunny Hug now.

You might want to give someone else a big Bunny Hug...can you think of anyone?

Exercise #10
Courage

It takes great courage to learn something new...and do something that is very difficult. By doing this lesson, you had great courage and Calm Cottontail and your new friend, Luna Moth are very proud of you!

Do the Courage Stretch – be proud!!!!

Calm Cottontail
Peace Lesson Plan

Quick Calming Tips

Lavender Wand
When you wave the lavender wand, children will know it's time to go their peaceful garden and relax.

Bunny Breath Breaths
These can be done anytime, anywhere. Have children close their eyes and imagine that they are breathing in the Garden Heliotrope flower.

Calm Cottontail Stretch
Take time to do the Calm Cottontail Peace Stretch during the day.

Bunny Whisperer
Remember to take time to spread peace to others today. Think of your friend, Luna Moth.

Bridge of Dreams
Remember to leave your problems behind before you move on.

Moonbeam Rides
Give children a light blue pompom to remind them of peace during the day.

Moonlight Serenades
Take time to listen to Nature CD and say affirmation throughout the day.
"I am peaceful. I am peaceful." Remember to look for the Bunny Blossoms.

Calm Cottontail Bunny
Let's send some peaceful thoughts to Calm Cottontail right now.
Hold Calm Cottontail and give him a Bunny Hug.

Courage
Take time to do the courage stretch whenever you are feeling worried or scared.
Remember you can do anything!

Peace

GARDEN HELIOTROPE

125

Calm Cottontail
Thoughts Lesson Plan

Exercise #1
Entering the Peaceful Garden

- Sit with legs crossed and eyes closed.
- Use Lavender Wand

We're getting ready to enter our peaceful garden….close your eyes, relax and let happy thoughts come into your mind. We are choosing to only let happy thoughts come our way right now.

Calm Cottontail is going to meet us in the garden. Rabbits can do so many amazing things – and jumping is one of them. They kick their back legs, which are very long and it helps them to jump. For such a little animal, they can go a long way and look pretty amazing jumping across the garden. This is just like our thoughts – they can jump from thing to thing. Some of our thoughts are sad or worried, but others can be happy and cheerful. Let's jump in our thoughts right now and make them all happy!

Say together:
   "I am going to my peaceful garden where I will only think happy thoughts."

Calm Cottontail
Thoughts Lesson Plan

Exercise #2
Bunny Breath Breaths

- Sit with their legs crossed or on knees.

Calm Cottontail is sitting under the Midnight Candy flower. This amazing flower grows in South Africa. It has maroon (dark pinkish/red) buds in the day, and at night, opens up with pure white flowers with heart shaped petals.

This flower can remind us that good thoughts are always inside of us – we just have to look deep inside.

Calm Cottontail says by doing your breathing, you can keep positive thoughts coming your way.

Breath in – smelling this flower, I start thinking happy thoughts.
Breath out – I send those happy thoughts out to the world.

- Repeat breathing 5-10 times...slow & deep

Other Breathing Suggestions:
- Parent or Teacher can suggest positive words to the child to think about while doing the Bunny Breath Breaths:
  - My favorite dream
  - My favorite animal
  - My favorite hobby
  - My favorite fun activity

127

Calm Cottontail
Thoughts Lesson Plan

Exercise #3
Calm Cottontail Stretch

• Get comfortable – remove shoes and be on a nonslid surface.

Calm Cottontail is going to show you how to take time to work on your thoughts.

Instructions for the stretch:

Lay on back with legs straight out on the ground. Slowly bend right knee in, grabbing toes with your right hand. Slowly try to stretch your leg up – as far as you can without discomfort. Keep your other leg flat on the ground. Then slowly stretch your right leg out to one side – trying to place it on the ground as far as you can go without discomfort. Then switch sides and do the same with the left leg.

• Rest in this pose for 10 seconds to start...then longer.

As you do this stretch, imagine lying with Calm Cottontail in the middle of your peaceful garden. Every time you stretch your leg up and down, think another happy thought. These happy thoughts are flowing to you...one right after another...and you can do this anytime.

-   What thoughts are coming to you? How do you feel?

Calm Cottontails
Thoughts Lesson Plan

Exercise #4
Bunny Whisperer

- **Sit in a comfortable position.**

Calm Cottontail wants to introduce you to his friend, the Mockingbird. This is an amazing bird, who loves to sing at night! This bird can sing 39 different songs and 50 different calls, but the most amazing thing, it can mimic other animals – it can even bark like a dog!

- Show the child a photo of a real Mockingbird.

- Have children close their eyes.

Calm Cottontail says that you can learn to talk to all of his friends in the Peaceful Garden…that you can become the Bunny Whisperer. All you have to do is keep your eyes closed, imagine walking up to the Mockingbird. What would you like to ask him? Take a long look at him – what would you like to name him?

- Practice talking like the Bunny Whisperer… What would you like to talk about today?

Calm Cottontails
Thoughts Lesson Plan

Exercise #5
Bridge of Dreams

- **Sit with legs crossed and eyes closed.**

Calm Cottontail shows you the bridge of dreams…it is here that you can ask for anything. Keep your eyes closed and think about what you want to wish for today….

Before you can walk across the bridge, you must promise to only think good thoughts. As you begin to walk across the bridge, you are feeling so happy – you are thinking about things that make you feel good and bring back good memories. You new friend, the Mockingbird is flying next to you.

When you get to the other side of the bridge, you all celebrate by dancing in the moonlight – Calm Cottontail loves to dance when he's happy! Kick up those big feet and jump all around!

- To have some fun, you can dance around the room – it will feel good!

- You can also have a <u>Midnight Tea Party</u> – who would you invite?

Calm Cottontails
Thoughts Lesson Plan

Exercise #6
Moonbeam Rides

- Sit with legs crossed and eyes closed.

The peaceful garden is turning yellow…keep your eyes closed and imagine seeing this color all around you. As you look at Calm Cottontail, he is also changing – his cottontail is turning yellow – can you see it? This reminds us, that we can also change – we can change how we feel at any moment. Right now, let's open our mind to happy thoughts…what makes you smile…what makes you happy?

You see a yellow moonbeam coming your way – you, Calm Cottontail and Mockingbird all jump on. The next time you are worried or angry or thinking negative thoughts, remember what we did here…remember that you can change your thoughts at any time. You watch your problems disappear into the night sky…one by one. Close your eyes and watch this…

On the moonbeam is the softest bed of forest moss and beautiful ferns acting as a blanket. You lay your head down and hear the song of the Mockingbird…it's so beautiful. As you listen more carefully, the song keeps changing…the Mockingbird can sing so many wonderful songs…they keep playing over and over again in our mind – bringing happy memories to you.

- You can give the children a yellow pompom, so they will remember to take time to listen all day.

131

Calm Cottontail
Thoughts Lesson Plan

Exercise #7
Moonlight Serenade

- Sit in a comfortable position.

As the moonbeam goes over the trees, you hear the music of the night – birds singing, crickets chirping – take time to listen. It's like a beautiful Moonlight Serenade.

- It's your turn to sing now:

  "I am happy.   I am happy."
   Can you hear the birds singing it with you?

You can sing this serenade anytime you are lonely or don't know what to say to someone. By singing this song, you are sending peace out to the whole world.

Bunny Blossoms
Every time you sing this song, it wakes up all the flowers in the garden. And if you look very closely, you can see them all turning into little Bunny Blossoms – they are all taking the shape of little bunnies...and showing you that anything is possible!

- Play a nature CD for relaxation at this time.

Calm Cottontail
Thoughts Lesson Plan

Exercise #8
Landing back in the Enchanted Garden

• **Lay down with eye pillow.**

You smell the Midnight Candy flower again – breathe in the beautiful fragrance, breathe out into the night sky.

Sometimes we think sad or angry thoughts. We know we can make these feelings drift away, by thinking happy thoughts.

Let's take a walk in our peaceful garden. You find a very quiet spot and lay your head down. Your mind is racing with thoughts – you have worries and problems and you want to send them away. Lying next to you is a very unique flower – it's all blue and glowing. As you pick it up, you see that inside there's an entire city inside the flower. As you look closer, you see amazing sights – parks and playgrounds, friends and animals...it's a beautiful sight. You realize that your mind is the same way – it's filled with so many amazing things – including happy, beautiful thoughts that you can see at any time. As you continue to hold this special blue flower, you drift off to sleep...thinking about a happy time you just remembered.

<u>Calm Cottontail</u>
Thoughts Lesson Plan

<u>Exercise #9</u>
Bunny Hugs

- Have a Calm Cottontail Bunny with you now.

You are thinking happy thoughts...they make you feel good. Calm Cottontail helped you and you're going to give him a big Bunny Hug now.

You might want to give someone else a big Bunny Hug...can you think of anyone?

<u>Exercise #10</u>
Courage

It takes great courage to learn something new...and do something that is very difficult. By doing this lesson, you had great courage and Calm Cottontail and your new friend, Mockingbird are very proud of you!

Do the Courage Stretch – be proud!!!!

Calm Cottontail
Thoughts Lesson Plan

Quick Calming Tips

Lavender Wand
When you wave the lavender wand, children will know it's time to think happy thoughts.

Bunny Breath Breaths
These can be done anytime, anywhere. Have children close their eyes and imagine that they are breathing in the Midnight Candy flower.

Calm Cottontail Stretch
Take time to do the Calm Cottontail Thoughts Stretch during the day.

Bunny Whisperer
Remember to take time to think happy thoughts today. Think of your friend, the Mockingbird.

Bridge of Dreams
Remember to leave your problems behind before you move on

Moonbeam Rides
Give children a yellow pompom to remind them of happy thoughts during the day.

Moonlight Serenades
Take time to listen to Nature CD and say affirmation throughout the day.
"I am happy." I am happy." Remember to look for the Bunny Blossoms.

Calm Cottontail Bunny
Let's send some good thoughts to Calm Cottontail...can you when he received them? Hold Calm Cottontail and give him a Bunny Hug.

Courage
Take time to do the courage stretch whenever you are feeling worried or scared. Remember you can do anything!

Thoughts

MIDNIGHT CANDY

Calm Cottontails
About the Author, Christi Eley

Christi Eley is the Founder of Angel Bear Yoga®, an international children's yoga program that is for children ages 3-10. Angel Bear Yoga focuses on the mind, body and spirit in an innovative way. Angel Bear lives in a magical forest where anything is possible. He teaches children positive character traits through the beauty of nature and yoga. He sees the angel in all children, providing opportunities for them to earn their wings, and make the world a better place.

Christi does many trainings and workshops throughout the year promoting this message. She has worked with the National Association for the Education of Young Children, Montessori Associations and Schools, yoga studios, and many parents throughout the world.

She is very active in her local community teaching weekly classes, holding special events, and working closely with the Children's Museum of Winston-Salem. She also promotes her Calm Cottontail Program - sharing her love of animals with young ones combining Humane Education and yoga. She is the mother of two wonderful daughters - Erin & Sydney, who she home schools and they share a menagerie of pets together!

Her trainings include: YogaKids Certification, International Yoga Training Program, YogaEd, Certification Program for Yoga in Schools, Itsy Bitsy Yoga Trained, Prenatal/Postnatal Yoga Training, Infant Massage Certification.

Check out her websites at:
www.angelbearyoga.com
www.cottontailandfriends.com

Calm Cottontails
About the Illustrator, Aries Cheung

Aries Cheung was born in Hong Kong and studied graphic design and illustration at the Hong Kong Polytechnics University. He moved to Canada in 1989 and received his BFA from York University. A professional illustrator and visual artist for twenty years, he specializes in oil, watercolor, pencil and digital media. His illustrations have appeared in books, magazines, television and advertising. His art has been exhibited in solo and group shows in Hong Kong and Canada. He was a member of the Canadian Society of Children's Authors, Illustrators and Performers, and was an art grant jury member for the Toronto Arts Council in 2000. Aries often goes beyond realism, exploring other art styles, such as surrealism and expressionism. He is particularly interested in creating visually experimental and whimsical characters for children. He has illustrated a number of children's books for various publishers in Canada and USA. He has facilitated public school students in the making of art, crafts and art quilt, and has taught art to adults and children. Trained and working also as a performing artist, he has performed for various dance and theatre companies. He has conducted workshops in art, mime and acting for schools and community organizations. Aries lives in Toronto, frequently contributing his artistic skills to non-profit cultural organizations and community events. He has taught at the Center for Creative Communications at the Centennial College in Toronto.

Check out his website at:
www.ariescheung.com

Check out the complete product line for
Angel Bear Yoga®
www.angelbearyoga.com

Books
CD's
DVD's
Accessories
Downloadable Lesson Plans
Trainings

Please feel free to contact us
with any questions or comments:
angelbearyoga@bellsouth.net

LaVergne, TN USA
09 June 2010
185615LV00002B/1/P